Wild Animals and Birds of South Africa

Written and illustrated by

Oliver T. Spedding

Copyright 2013 Oliver T. Spedding

CHACMA BABOON (PAPIO URSINUS)

SIZE: Baboon males reach a head and body length of between 100 and 110 cms and weigh about 32 kgs. Tails can reach a length of 70 cms.

DESCRIPTION: Baboons range in colour from dark brown to dark grey with a great deal of longer black hair on the body. The tail is carried with the first third held upwards and the other two thirds hanging downwards. Adult males have a mane of long hair on the back of the neck and shoulders.

FOOD: Baboons eat a wide range of vegetable matter and insects. Grasses, seeds, roots, bulbs, leaves, flowers, bark, gum, mushrooms, wild flowers, pods, shoots, spiders, scorpions, ants and even slugs are all food for baboons.

Regular access to drinking water is essential to the survival of the baboon.

BUFFALO (SYNCERUS CAFFER)

SIZE: The buffalo male stands about 140 cms at the shoulder and weighs up to 800 kgs.

DESCRIPTION: Buffalo are large, heavily built, ox-like animals ranging in colour from reddish-brown to black. The horns of the old males are massive. Young buffalo are well haired, but adults have a very sparse coating. Ears are large and tipped with hair, the muzzle is broad and usually shiny while the tail is long and has a tuft of black or dark brown hair at the tip.

FOOD: Buffalo are predominantly grazers but will occasionally browse. Fresh, sprouting young grass is attractive to them but they will readily feed on old grass.

Buffalo occur in herds of several thousand and they are reputed to be the most dangerous African species to hunt.

CHEETAH (ACINONYX JUBATUS)

SIZE: From the tip of the nose to the tip of the tail the cheetah is about 2 m long. They stand about 80 cms at the shoulder and weigh about 50 kgs.

DESCRIPTION: Cheetah are very elegant and have beautiful spotted coats. They are tall and slender and have long tails. The cheetah has a rounded head, very short muzzle and small rounded ears. They have very distinctive "tear marks" curving from the inner corners of the eyes to the corners of the mouth.

FOOD: Cheetah are solitary hunters of prey weighing up to 60 kgs. They prefer young buck, zebra and giraffe and small mammals such as guinea fowl, bustards, porcupine and hares.

Cheetah are considered the fastest animals on earth over short distances and achieve speeds of up to 75 km per hour for distances from 100 - 300 m.

ELAND (TAUROTRAGUS ORYX)

SIZE: The largest of the African antelope, the adult male Eland stands about 1,7 m at the shoulder and weighs up to 700 kgs.

DESCRIPTION: Eland vary in colour from light fawn to dun and usually have narrow white stripes down their flanks. The males have heavier horns than females and the world record for a pair of Eland horns is 102,3 cms.

FOOD: Eland prefer to browse but during the summer months graze considerably. They use their horns to break branches so that they can reach the green leaves.

Eland are timid animals and are quick to gallop off if disturbed. If a fence blocks their way, they will approach it slowly, pause, and then jump, easily clearing 2 m.

ELEPHANT (LOXODONTA AFRICANA)

SIZE: The elephant has the highest shoulder height of all mammals, the highest recorded height being 4 m. Adult males weigh between 5 550 kgs and 6 00kgs. The heaviest pair of tusks on record weighed 102,3 kgs and 97 kgs.

DESCRIPTION: The skin colour of elephants is grey or brownish-grey. The ear flaps are very large and can reach a vertical height of 2 m and are flapped to create air currents over the blood vessels thus cooling the body temperature. The main feature of the species is undoubtedly the trunk which is extremely versatile. The moth is small and spout-shaped.

FOOD: Elephants browse and graze and will also eat the bark of certain trees. Elephants need about 300 kgs of green food and 160 litres of water daily.

Elephants are extremely destructive and when entering a small woodland have been known to destroy up to two thirds of the trees.

GIRAFFE (GIRAFFA CAMELOPARDALIS)

SIZE: The average height of a male giraffe is between 4,9 m and 5,2 m and the average weight is 1 200 kgs.

DESCRIPTION: The body of the giraffe is large with irregularly shaped patches of dark brown colour divided by lighter-coloured bands. The lower parts of the legs are usually white. The tops of the two "horns" are covered with black hair and giraffe have a mane of stiff brush-like black hair down the back of their long necks.

FOOD: Giraffe are browsers but will occasionally graze on fresh palatable grasses.

Because of their long necks, giraffe cannot scratch the sides of their heads and necks with their hind legs as other animals do, so they rub against trees and other tall objects to relieve irritation.

HIPPOPOTAMUS (HIPPOPOTAMUS AMPHIBIUS)

SIZE: Hippopotamus males reach a weight of 2 000 kgs and stand about 1,5 m at the shoulder. Calves weigh about 60 kgs at birth.

DESCRIPTION: Hippopotamus have barrel-shaped bodies, short stout legs, broad heads and smooth naked skin. Their mouths are very large and wide and their eyes raised on bony protuberances on the top of the head. The body is grey-black in colour with a pink tinge.

FOOD: Hippopotamus are grazers and eat up to 130 kgs of green grass per full feed. They can cause great damage on riverside farms as they are notorious crop raiders.

Hippopotamus walk on the bottom of deep pools and tend to use the same paths which become clearly marked on the sandy bottom. They can remain under water for 5 to 6 minutes.

SPOTTED HYAENA (CROCUTA CROCUTA)

SIZE: Adult hyaena stand about 80 cms at the shoulder and weigh about 80 kgs.

DESCRIPTION: Spotted hyaena have very heavy fore quarters and lighter hind quarters. The head is broad and large with rounded ears. The body is usually ground colour and covered with dark brown irregularly distributed spots. When running, with their tails between their legs, they give the impression of having very sloping backs.

FOOD: Spotted Hyaena prey on most medium-sized hoofed animals. Once a kill is made it is consumed in a remarkably short time. 35 hyaena are known to have eaten a zebra weighing 220 kgs and its foal weighing 150 kgs in just 35 minutes.

When chasing prey, spotted hyaena can gallop at speeds of 40 to 50 kms per hour for 4 to 5 kms.

IMPALA (AEPYCEROS MELAMPUS)

SIZE: Impala males stand about 90 cms at the shoulder and weigh up to 50 kgs. The world record for a pair of impala horns is 80,97 cms.

DESCRIPTION: One of the most beautiful and graceful of the African antelope, the impala has a shiny reddish coat and long slender legs. The under parts are white. Only the males carry horns which are strongly ridged for the bottom two thirds.

FOOD: Impala browse and graze, depending on the vegetation and the season. They are also partial to wild fruits. Impala are dependent on water for drinking and usually stay within 8 kms of permanent water sources.

Impala are very fleet of foot and run with graceful leaps of up to 12 m.

KUDU (TRAGELAPHUS STREPSICEROS)

SIZE: Adult male kudu stand about 1,4 m at the shoulder and weigh up to 250 kgs. The world record for a pair of kudu horns is 181,6 cms.

DESCRIPTION: The body colour of the kudu is fawn-grey and they have a series of six to ten white stripes across their backs. The shoulders of both males and females have distinct humps. Kudu have upstanding manes and their tails are blackish above and white underneath. Their ears are particularly large and broad and adult males have short beards and a fringe of long hair running down the throat and upper chest to the mid-belly.

FOOD: Kudu are browsers, although on rare occasions they may eat fresh grass. They also eat seed pods either green or dry. Kudu are very destructive raiders of cultivated crops.
Kudu are great jumpers and fences must be at least 3 m high to prevent crops being raided.

LEOPARD (PANTHERA PARDUS)

SIZE: The largest of the African spotted cats, the leopard measures about 2,9 m from the tip of its nose to the tip of its tail. The average weight of a fully grown male is 60 kgs.

DESCRIPTION: Leopards have black spots on the limbs, flanks, head and hind quarters and rosettes on the rest of the body. The ground colour varies from off-white to golden. The hair is short over the whole body, never longer than 30 mm. Ears are small and rounded and the white whiskers are particularly long.

FOOD: Leopards will hunt ant prey from mice to mammals twice their size and also catch fish. They will also take birds from doves to ostriches, porcupines and even lizards and snakes.

Leopards are expert swimmers and take to water readily. They are secretive animals and hunt by stalking their prey.

LION (PANTHERA LEO)

SIZE: Lion males stand up to 1,25 m at the shoulder and weigh up to 240 kgs.

DESCRIPTION: Lions are generally tawny on the upper parts and white on the under parts. Adult males have a mane of long hair about 15 cms in length for protection when fighting. The backs of the rounded ears are black and the tail has a tuft of long hair at the tip.

FOOD: Lions feed on mammals from mice to buffalo, birds, reptiles and even insects. Lions will take carrion and also fish when these can be easily obtained in drying up pools. The males take little part in the hunt but usually feed first once the prey has been taken.
In the absence of their normal prey, lions can become problem animals and can cause great losses of cattle and other livestock and may even become 'man eaters".

RHINOCEROS (RHINOCEROTIDAE)

SQUARE-LIPPED RHINOCEROS

SIZE: Square-lipped rhinoceros have a shoulder height of about 180 cms and weigh between 2 000 and 2 300 kgs. The record length of a front horn is 158 cms.

DESCRIPTION: The skin is grey in colour and may reach a thickness of 2 cms. The lips are square which enables this species to crop grass to within 1 cm of the ground. The front horn is invariably longer than the hind.

FOOD: Square-lipped rhinoceros are grazers with a bite width of about 20 cms and nearly half of daylight hours are taken up in feeding.

HOOK-LIPPED RHINOSCEROS

SIZE: Hooked-lipped rhinoceros have a shoulder height of about 160 cms and weigh up to 1 000 kgs. The longest recorded horn is 120 cms.

DESCRIPTION: The skin is dark grey in colour and the upper lip is prehensile (capable of grasping). The front horn is invariably longer than the hind.

FOOD: Hook-lipped rhinoceros are browsers and manoeuvre food into their mouths with their upper lip.

SPRINGBOK (ANTIDORCAS MARSUPIALIS)

SIZE: Springbok stand about 75 cms at the shoulder and weigh about 40 kgs. The longest male horns on record measured 49,22 cms.

DESCRIPTION: The upper parts of the springbok are bright cinnamon-brown and are separated from the pure white under parts by a dark reddish-brown horizontal band. The horns of the females are distinctly smaller than those of the males. The tails are white with a tuft of black hair at the tip. The face is white and the ears are outstandingly long.

FOOD: Springbok browse and graze. In winter or dry months they browse on the leaves of trees and shrubs and grass is of little importance. However, in the summer months a great deal more grass is eaten.

The springbok can run at up to 70 kms per hour and when alarmed can leap up to 2 m off the ground.

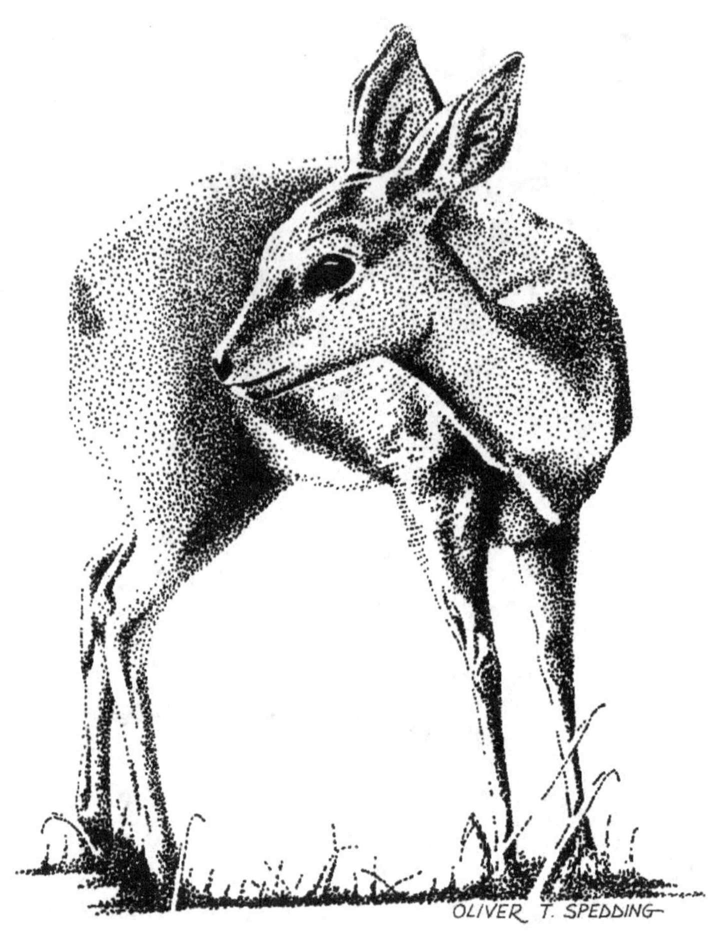

STEENBOK (RAPHICERUS CAMPESTRIS)

SIZE: Steenbok stand about 52 cms at the shoulder and weigh about 11 kgs. The world record for a pair of steenbok horns is 19,05 cms.

DESCRIPTION: Steenbok are small, graceful antelope with long slender legs. They are usually light brown in colour on the upper parts and white on the under parts. The ears are very large and only the males have horns.

FOOD: Steenbok browse as well as graze. Although they are known to drink, they are independent of drinking water and can obtain their moisture requirements from their food.

VERVET MONKEY (CERCOPITHECUS PYGERYTHRUS)

SIZE: Vervet monkeys have a head and body length of about 49 cms and a tail length of about 65 cms. They weigh about 30 kgs.

DESCRIPTION: The upper parts of the body, from the forehead to the base of the tail are grizzled grey. The face is covered with short black hair and the hands are black. The tail tends to darken towards the tip. The under parts are whitish.

FOOD: Vervet monkeys are mainly vegetarians, living on wild fruits, leaves, seeds and seed pods. They also occasionally eat insects. They very rarely swallow food directly after chewing and usually store the chewed food in the cheek pouches. Only when these pouches are full does swallowing start.

WARTHOG (PHACOCHOERUS AETHIOPICUS)

SIZE: The adult boar stands about 70 cms at the shoulder and weighs up to 100 kgs.

DESCRIPTION: Warthogs are grey in colour and have a crest of long hair running from the top of the head to the base of the tail. They have large "warts" on their faces which are actually outgrowths of skin.

FOOD: Warthogs are vegetarians and graze on short grass, herbs, shrubs, wild fruit and roots. They dig up roots by kneeling on the front legs and using the upper edge of the hard snout as a digging tool.

Warthogs live in holes dug by ant bears which the adults enter backwards. They love to wallow in mud which protects them against biting flies. When disturbed warthogs trot off with their tails held vertically.

WATERBUCK (KOBUS ELLIPSIPRYMNUS)

SIZE: Waterbuck are large antelope, the males standing 1,7 m at the shoulder and weighing between 250 and 270 kgs. Only the male waterbuck have horns and the world record for a pair of waterbuck horns is 99,7 cms.

DESCRIPTION: The upper parts of the body are dark brown-grey grizzled with grey and white hairs. They have a broad white ring around the rump, white patches above the eyes and a white ring around the top of the muzzle. The ears are short and the horns are heavily ringed.

FOOD: Waterbuck are grazers but occasionally browse plants. They eat most types of grass including reeds.

As their name implies, waterbuck are mostly found near vleis, rivers and even near artificial water supplies such as boreholes and pumps.

BLUE WILDEBEEST (CONNOCHAETES TAURINUS)

SIZE: Blue wildebeest males stand about 150 cms at the shoulder and weigh about 250 kgs. The world record for a pair of blue wildebeest horns, at their greatest width is 83,8 cms.

DESCRIPTION: Adult blue wildebeest are dark grey in colour with a silvery sheen and look almost black at a distance. The shoulders are humped and the heads are massive, making their legs look slender. Their chins have a distinct beard of long black hair. Both males and females carry unridged horns.

FOOD: Blue wildebeest are grazers and prefer feeding in areas of short, green grassland. They rarely eat grass that is more than 10 to 15 cms high.

A mass movement of blue wildebeest 16 kms long and about 10 kms wide was recorded in 1980.

AFRICAN WILD DOG (LYCAON PICTUS)

SIZE: Adults weigh between 18 and 36 kgs and males stand about 75 cms at the shoulder. The head and body length ranges between 75 and 140 cms and the tail length is between 30 and 45 cms.

DESCRIPTION: Known as the "painted dog", the African wild dog has a massive jaw, very large bat-like ears and, unlike wolves and domestic dogs which have five toes, have only four toes on each foot. Their mottled coats are colourful, made up of dark brown, black and yellow patches. The tail is bushy with a white tip.

FOOD: Wild dogs prey on gazelles and other antelope, warthogs, wildebeest and zebra calves, rats and birds.

ZEBRA (EQUUS BURCHELLI)

SIZE: The Burchell's zebra stands about 136 cms at the shoulder and weighs around 320 kgs.

DESCRIPTION: Zebra are easily recognised by their characteristic stripes and no two individuals are exactly alike. The black striping is usually broader on the body and hind quarters than on the neck and head. The ears are upstanding with rounded tips. The mane is also upstanding and the tail has a tuft of long black hair at the tip.

FOOD: Burchell's zebra are predominantly grazers although they do occasionally browse.

Burchell's zebra are very partial to rolling in dust which tends to obscure the contrast in their stripes.

BATELEUR EAGLE (TERATHOPIUS ECAUDATUS)

SIZE: Adults are 55 to 70 cms in length with a wingspan of around 1.75 m and a weight of 1,8 to 2,9 kgs.

DESCRIPTION: Bateleur eagles have black plumage with a chestnut mantle and tail, grey shoulders and red facial skin, bill and legs. Their tails are noticeably short.

FOOD: Bateleur eagles prey mostly on birds such as pigeons and sand grouse. They also take small mammals and occasionally take carrion.

Bateleur eagles take up to eight years to reach full maturity and hunt over a territory of 650 square kilometres.

BEARDED VULTURE (GYPAETUS BARBATUS)

SIZE: Bearded vultures weigh around 5,7 kgs and have a wingspan up to 2,8 m.

DESCRIPTION: Unlike most vultures the bearded vulture doesn't have a bald head or neck. The feet are large and powerful. They are mostly dark grey, rusty and whitish with orange or rust around the head. Bristles under the chin form a distinctive black beard. Tail and wing feathers are often grey.

FOOD: Bearded vultures feed mainly on the remains of dead animals and 85-90% of their diet is bone marrow. To break the bones they carry them to a great height and drop them onto rocks below.

The bearded vulture has learnt to catch tortoises and break their shells by dropping them onto rocks from a great height.

BLACK EAGLE (AQUILA VERREAUXII)

SIZE: the black eagle has a body length of 75 - 96 cms and a wingspan of 1,80 - 2,2 m.

DESCRIPTION: These eagles are black with a distinct white V-marking on their backs.

FOOD: Black eagles are specialist hunters of dassies but occasionally prey on guinea fowl and large rodents.

Black eagles are highly territorial and mate for life. Their nests are usually situated on cliff ledges.

CRESTED GUINEA FOWL (GUTTERA PUCHERANI)

SIZE: Crested guinea fowl have a length of about 50 cms, a wing length of 26 cms and weigh about 1,3 kgs.

DESCRIPTION: Crested guinea fowl are roughly the size of a domestic chicken, slate-grey in colour and finely spotted in white. They have a noticeably curly black crest on the head.

FOOD: Crested guinea fowl eat seeds, fruit, berries, roots, corms, insects and snails.

These birds often follow troops of monkeys to feed on fallen fruit.

AFRICAN FISH EAGLE (HALIAEETUS VOCIFER)
SIZE: The females are larger than the males weighing from 3,2 to 3,6 kgs and having a wingspan of about 2,4 m. Body length is 63 to 75 cms.
DESCRIPTION: The body is mostly brown with large, powerful black wings. The head, breast and tail are snow white and the featherless face is yellow. The hook-shaped beak is yellow with a black tip.
 FOOD: These birds feed mainly on fish but will also take waterfowl, small turtles, baby crocodiles, flamingos, lizards and frogs.

GIANT EAGLE OWL (BUBO LACTEUS)

SIZE: Africa's largest owl, the giant eagle owl has a body length of 60 - 66 cms, a wingspan of around 1,4 m and weighs from 1,6 to 2,0 kgs.

DESCRIPTION: The body is fairly uniform brownish-grey with light vermiculations and white spots on the shoulders. They have a whitish oval face with a black border. Eyes are orange and they have two fluffy ear-tufts.

FOOD: Giant eagle owls feed on large birds and medium-sized mammals including monkeys, hares, mongoose, squirrels, fruit bats, rats and mice.

Giant eagle owls are nocturnal birds that roost in trees and are near the top of the food chain so have no natural predators.

HAMERKOP (SCOPUS UMBRETTA)

SIZE: Hamerkop have a length of about 56 cms, a wingspan of 90 to 94 cms and weigh from 425 to 430 grams.

DESCRIPTION: Hamerkop are dark brown with a black bill, legs and feet. The large bill and crest give the hammerhead appearance and the legs are moderately long.

FOOD: Hamerkop eat tadpoles, frogs and small fish. They forage by wading in shallow water, stirring the mud with their feet and often fly slowly over the water and snatch food from the surface with their bills.

HELMETED GUINEA FOWL (NUMIDA MELEAGRIS)

SIZE: Helmeted guinea fowl have a length of about 55 cms, a wing length of about 27 cms and weigh between 1,14 and 1,86 kgs.

DESCRIPTION: Helmeted guinea fowl are about the size of a large domestic chicken, slate grey in colour and finely spotted in white. The head is naked, red and blue and has a conspicuous horny casque on top. The legs and feet are black.

FOOD: Helmeted guinea fowl eat seeds, bulbs, tubers, berries, insects, snails, ticks and millipedes.

These birds can run very fast when disturbed, fly very well and when approaching a waterhole the flock will walk in single file.

HOOPOE (UPUPA EPOPS)

SIZE: Hoopoe have a length of 25 to 27 cms, a wingspan of about 38 cms and weigh from 57 to 67 grams.

DESCRIPTION: The back and under parts of the hoopoe are bright orange-brown and the wings are boldly barred in black and white. The bill is long and curves slightly downward. Hoopoe have a very distinctive crest which is erected into a fan shape when the bird is alarmed.

FOOD: Hoopoe feed on insects such as cutworms, earthworms, small snakes and small frogs. They forage by walking on the ground with short quick steps and nodding their heads as they probe the ground with their bills.

YELLOW BILLED HORNBILL (TOCKUS FLAVIROSTRIS)

SIZE: Yellow billed hornbills have a length of about 54 cms, a wing length of around 20 cms and weigh about 210 grams.

DESCRIPTION: Yellow billed hornbills have large yellow-orange bills which curve slightly downward, wings that are boldly mottled black and white and longish black tails. Their legs and feet are black and their eyes yellow.

FOOD: Yellow billed hornbills feed on rodents, insects, scorpions, solifugids, centipedes, seeds and fruit.

MARTIAL EAGLE (POLEMAETUS ELAUDATUS)

SIZE: The largest of the African eagles, the martial eagle weighs around 6,5 kgs and has a wingspan of about 2 m.

DESCRIPTION: The upper parts of the body are dark brown and the belly is white with black streaks. The legs are white with large talons.

FOOD: Birds are an important part of the martial eagle's diet and include guinea fowl, francolins, bustards and poultry. They also take small antelope and domestic goats and lambs.

The martial eagle is very powerful and is capable of knocking an adult man off his feet.

OSTRICH (STRUTHIO CAMELUS)

SIZE: Ostrich males stand up to 2 m high, have a wing length of about 90 cms and weigh from 59 to 81 kgs.

DESCRIPTION: Ostrich are very large birds, the males mostly black with white wings and a buff tail and females brownish-grey. The neck is very long and nearly naked as are the long legs.

FOOD: The main food of the ostrich is grass, berries, seeds, succulent plants, small reptiles and insects.

The ostrich can run at speeds of 50 to 60 kms per hour.

SECRETARY BIRD (SAGITTARIUS SERPENTARIUS)

SIZE: Secretary birds have a length of about 140 cms, a wing length of about 65 cms and weigh between 3,4 and 4,3 kgs.

DESCRIPTION: Secretary birds have long legs and tail and are grey in colour on the body, neck and head. The rump and crest feathers are black as are the feathers on the upper leg. The face is bright orange and the legs are greyish-pink.

FOOD: The main food of the secretary bird consists of insects, small amphibians, lizards, snakes, rodents, young hares, small birds and eggs.